The JOY of GRILL PIZZA

Dominick Bosco

Former Senior Editor Prevention Magazine

Story Hill Books

Story Hill Books
DB@StoryHillBooks.com
www.StoryHillBooks.com

ISBN 13: 978-0-9841907-2-0

ISBN 10:   0-9841907-2-4

Library of Congress Control Number: 2010905210
Printed in the United States of America

First Edition

Although the author and publisher have made every effort to ensure that the information in this book was correct at press time, the author and publisher do not assume and hereby disclaim any liability to any party for any loss, damage, or disruption caused by errors or omissions, whether such errors or omissions result from negligence, accident, or any other cause.

CKB064000 COOKING / Courses & Dishes / Pizza
CKB005000 COOKING / Methods / Barbecue & Grilling
CKB029000 COOKING / Entertaining

For my father,

who showed me the joy of cooking for a crowd

Contents

The Grill Pizza Revolution Is HERE!

The book you are holding in your hands is not a cookbook. It is a manifesto for a revolution in the most popular food on the planet—pizza.

Forget your fancy brick ovens!

Forget ALL your ovens!

Turn your pizza stones into patios! You'll never need them again!

Forget your pilgrimages to New Haven and Brooklyn and Naples! You are only a few minutes from the best pizza you ever tasted.

This book is your ticket to Pizza Paradise. The Happy Hunting Ground for pizza is in your own backyard.

The Best Pizza You Ever Tasted ... In 10 Minutes!

If you're not making pizza on your grill, you're missing out on something wonderful, because ...

Grill pizza is the best-tasting pizza you'll ever MAKE— and the best-tasting pizza you'll ever EAT!

Wait a second ... am I saying that YOU can make a pizza that's BETTER than New York pizza? BETTER than New Haven pizza? BETTER than Naples pizza?

Yes, I am. And yes, you will.

In fact, if you spent a month in New York City and ate nothing but pizza for breakfast, lunch, dinner, and midnight snacks at a different pizza restaurant every time—you wouldn't find a pizza that tastes better than the pizzas I'll show you how to make in your own backyard.

And if you made a month-long pizza pilgrimage to Italy, including two weeks in Naples, where pizza was invented, the pizzas you will make following the easier-than-pizza-pie steps in this book will taste BETTER!

This is no empty promise. I am NOT easy to please when it comes to pizza.

I was born in New HAVEN and grew up eating the best pizza this side of the Atlantic Ocean.

I've gone on that pizza pilgrimage to Italy and devoured pizzas from Venice and Florence to Rome and points south—including Naples and Sicily.

And when the waiter brought my first *Vera Pizza Napoletana* to the candlelit table in that romantic Naples alley, I was struck by how much it looked like the pizzas I make on my grill at home.

Real Naples Pizza

And as Neapolitan troubadors serenaded our table and I sliced the pizza, I was struck by how much the soft chewy texture felt exactly like the pizzas I make on my grill.

And when I experienced my first bite of genuine Naples pizza, at the restaurant that claimed a heritage dating back to the FIRST MARGHERITA PIZZA EVER, a pizza assembled from certified Italian ingredients by a chef trained by the best in the world, a pie baked in a wood-fired oven constructed to exacting specifications by Neapolitan oven-builders—Why, everyone who had ANYTHING at all to do with this pizza, from the farmers who grew the tomatoes to the apprentice who tended the oven fire, were ARTISANS among ARTISANS—I was really astonished!

Because it tasted ALMOST AS GOOD as the pizzas I make on the ten-year-old grill in my backyard!

We can argue about where to find the best pizza on earth—but only until you read this book and try it out for yourself. Because once you make pizza this unbelievably quick and easy way, there will not be any argument anymore.

The best pizza in the world will be at YOUR HOUSE!

Real
Grill Pizza

What *IS* Grill Pizza, Anyway?

B efore I go any further, I should explain what I mean by "grill pizza" and "making pizza on the grill."

I DON'T mean using a pizza stone or a cast iron griddle. These are fine tools but you don't need them!

I DON'T mean grilling the pizza for a few minutes and then "finishing" it in the oven. I'd call that "cheating" except it is NOT a shortcut to a better pizza. It's a shortcut to an INFERIOR pizza. I DO mean making a pizza on the grill that's in your yard right now—gas or charcoal. You don't need a special grill, special attachments, or special tools.

I DO mean making the pizza right on the grates.

WHOA! Won't the dough fall through?

No. In a decade of making grill pizza with all kinds of dough, this has NEVER happened to me.

WHOA! Won't the dough catch fire and burn?

N o—at least not any more often than your burgers, steaks, salmon, veggies, and hot dogs catch fire and burn.

Will you get that "pizza parlor flavor"?

NO. You'll get a pizza that tastes so good, you'll forget all about pizza parlor flavor. I live close to the best pizza parlors on earth and I rarely bother with them anymore.

But ... will you get authentic brick oven pizza flavor?
NO!

Your grill pizzas will taste BETTER than any pizza that comes out of a brick oven.

You'll get a smoky depth of flavor that ONLY A GRILL can impart to food! How do I know this?

I HAVE a brick oven!

And I discovered—after spending thousands of dollars to build it—that I can make better pizza on my ten-year-old gas grill!

Why did I spend all that money if I already knew I could make great pizza on my grill?

Because I'm human and I usually need to learn things the hard way.

And because, like any human, I get caught up in things that have a mystique. And wood-fired brick ovens have BONUS amounts of pure MYSTIQUE. I mean ... just the fact that in Italy your

The JOY of GRILL PIZZA!

backyard is positively NAKED without one is mystique enough, right?

The Moment I Learned
The Hard Way

It happened at one of my pizza parties. My pizza parties are NOT highly-organized affairs. They're kind of chaotic. Usually, little kids are poking sticks in the pond. Bigger kids are poking sticks in the pizza oven, trying to roast marshmallows. Adults are yakking and munching and ... you get the idea. Meanwhile, I'm bustling around making pizzas one after another.

One day, after several pizzas from the brick oven, I decided to give the oven a rest and make a pizza on the grill.

No one was paying attention to me. I made the grill pizza and just plopped it down on the pizza plate in the middle of the table, sliced it, and walked away to make another pizza as people were stuffing the new pizza into their mouths.

Then I heard the words that started the Grill Pizza Revolution, uttered in that unmistakable mouth-full-of-delicious-pizza voice:

"HEY, THIS IS THE BEST ONE YET!"

The JOY of GRILL PIZZA!

Huh?

Best one yet? You mean I've been making pizzas all afternoon in the brick oven and THE BEST ONE YET is the one I make on the ten-year-old gas grill?

You mean to say I hauled firewood, lit and tended the fire for two hours before the party and THE BEST PIZZA

YET is the one I plunked on the table ten minutes after switching on the gas grill?

I know, just ONE "best pizza yet" is not enough to deflate a mystique. But I kept having these *"That's the best pizza you ever made!"* moments—and always after I made a GRILL PIZZA.

So ... finally ... I learned my lesson: If you have a grill—gas or charcoal—you can make pizzas that can and will compete in the same league as the best pizzas made in a wood-burning pizza oven. In fact, your grill will give you incredible, irresistible flavors that YOU CANNOT GET in a wood-burning oven.

You will get a better crust on the grill, with less fuss and bother, than you EVER could in your electric or gas oven.

But ... you will also get a crust that can compete in flavor and texture with the BEST you can get out of a

The JOY of GRILL PIZZA!

wood-fired brick oven. The best pizza you ever make ... the best pizza you ever taste ... will come off your grill.

Call It "Grill Pizza"

It's "grill pizza" NOT "grilled pizza." Calling it "grilled pizza" doesn't say enough, as if the grill is just an accessory. You don't call pizza made in a brick oven "brick-ovened" pizza, do you?

Once you TASTE grill pizza, you'll get it. Making pizza on a grill gives the pizza a unique identity and flavor. It's GRILL PIZZA, not "pizza that just happened to have been grilled." The grill makes it what it is. It's a collection of ingredients that is transformed into a very delicious, very special, very unique pizza BY the grill. It's a grill pizza.

The Best-Kept Secret in the World

Grill pizza is the best kept secret in the world—and it shouldn't be, because it's not only the MOST FUN way to make a pizza, but also the EASIEST way to make an INCREDIBLY DELICIOUS pizza. A pizza that has people ooing and ahhing ...

A pizza that is wildly delicious ... a pizza that can compete with the best pizzas on earth.

BETTER than your favorite pizza parlor!

BETTER than the best take-out!

BETTER than the BEST pizza you ever ate!

You don't need a brick oven!

You don't need fancy ingredients!

You don't need tricky tools!

All you need is this book and your grill!

The Grill Pizza Challenge:

Make your best pizza in your brick oven, your kitchen oven, your restaurant oven, on a stone or in a pan.

Then use the SAME INGREDIENTS to make a grill pizza, following the easy steps in this book.

The grill pizza will taste BETTER!

Your First Grill Pizza!
The Classic Maggie

As the legend goes, the first pizza Margherita was a command performance. A Neapolitan baker created it in his oven to serve Queen Margherita of Savoy. To symbolize the Italian colors, he used red tomatoes, white cheese, and green basil. The queen liked it so much, the baker named it after her.

When your friends and family taste your first grill pizza, you'll be commanded to make more of them, too.

WARNING: Once the first bite of grill pizza starts to spread its hot, cheesy, tomato-y, bready wonderfulness in your mouth, you CAN'T GO BACK! You will NEVER be able to eat pizza ANYWHERE without KNOWING that YOU can make it BETTER in your own backyard. This is NOT a step you should take lightly. Warn your family and friends, too—especially the kids!

Tools You'll Need

ESSENTIAL

A grill. You can make a delicious grill pizza on ANY grill, gas or charcoal. As a rule, the hotter the grill, the more attentive you need to be because things happen faster on a hotter grill.

A grill spatula. After the grill, this is really the only essential tool. Even the smallest pizza is wider than the average burger, so flipping it over or keeping it level while lifting it off the grill can be very tricky (and messy!) if the business end of the spatula is not wide enough to balance the pizza.

NICE TO HAVE

A tray to carry all your tools and ingredients to the grill. Instead of throwing away that trusty old pizza pan, use it to ferry ingredients and tools to the grill.

An olive oil bottle with a pouring spout.

A knife, for last-second slicing of ingredients.

The JOY of GRILL PIZZA!

A cheese grater for when you need more shredded cheese.

A pizza platter. That pizza is going to be HOT AND JUICY when it comes off the grill!

A pizza cutter. The wheel cutter is fun. **Food scissors** can come in handy, too.

A pizza or cake pan that's the same diameter as the pizzas you want to make. You can shape dough on any oiled or floured surface, but using a pan as a "form" comes in handy when you want uniform shape and size.

Bowls, dishes, jars, and spoons for your ingredients.

A water spritzer for the occasional, ahem, moment when flaming olive oil joins with grill gunk you should have cleaned out last year and turns your grill into a caldron of doom.

INGREDIENTS

B efore talking about ingredients, this would be a good time to tell you:

Bosco's
Prime Pizza
Directive

Just GET IT DELICIOUS!

Use the ingredients that taste good to YOU! Go with the easiest and most convenient options that will give you the flavors you love.

In our quest for the Ultimate Pizza, things can get ridiculous. Where do you draw the line? Do you grow your own wheat for the flour to make the dough? Do you have a cow in the backyard so you can be in COMPLETE CONTROL of the cheese-making process? Do you grow your own tomatoes or simply take a field trip to Naples to inspect the vines before you order direct from the farmer?

Okay, if you have one of those restaurants where people pay $40 for a pizza, then maybe you have to convince them it's worth it by chasing down the most excruciatingly trendy ingredients on the planet. *Yes, we use ONLY cheese made with milk from water buffalo raised in the foothills of the Alps on organic heirloom grains grown above 5000 feet ... by nuns.*

But if you're making pizza for your family and friends and all you have to do is impress them with how good it tastes ... and if you can get an ingredient that really meets your specs for flavor and quality out of a can or the freezer section, then you don't need anyone's permission to DO IT!

And ... one more thing NEVER to forget when making grill pizza:

> ## The ONLY Universal Rule For Grill Pizza Ingredients:
> **All ingredients should be edible and near, at, or above room temperature at the time they go on top of the pizza.**

R eason: The only thing that's going to actually COOK on the grill is the dough. The cheese will melt. The oil will sizzle. The sauce will steam. The meat and veggies will get hot and maybe even a little singed. But nothing except the dough will cook. So any ingredient that can't be normally eaten raw must be completely cooked BEFORE it goes on the pizza.

Okay, enough rules already! Here are the ingredients for your FIRST GRILL PIZZA:

THE CLASSIC MAGGIE—QUEEN OF APIZZA

8 oz fresh mozzarella, sliced

1/2 cup crushed tomatoes (see tomatoes below)

drizzle olive oil

garlic powder to taste

sprinkle rosemary (fresh or dried)

grated cheese

fresh basil

EXTRA VIRGIN OLIVE OIL!

Extra virgin olive oil is one of the prime ingredients of a good pizza, whether it's a grill pizza, a brick oven pizza, or a pan pizza. Bathe your dough in it, drizzle it on top and along the edge while the pizza is cooking and watch the flames flare!

Look for olive oil that has the words "first cold pressed" on the label. No need to get a second mortgage to buy it, either. When it goes on sale, stock up.

For sweet, dessert pizzas, use light olive oil, brush on melted butter, or use no oil at all.

DOUGH!

I could write a whole book about dough. But since the purpose of this book is to get a bite of delicious grill pizza melting in your mouth as soon as possible, I'm not going to get into dough making. If you make your own dough, there's no reason why you can't use it for grill pizza.

If you don't make your own dough, there are plenty of places to get pizza dough. A decade ago, pizza dough was rare in supermarkets and the only option was frozen bread dough (which is still a good choice). Nowadays, just about every supermarket sells pizza dough.

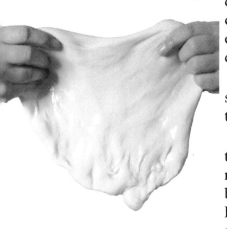

Most pizza restaurants will sell you some of their dough, too, bless their hearts.

I recommend taking the thawed dough out of the refrigerator at least 2 hours before you want to make pizza. If the dough is too cold, it'll be really difficult to spread into shape. You want it around room temperature. In fact, if the dough is too tight to spread, you can even microwave it on the very lowest setting for a minute or two to soften it.

In an emergency, you can thaw a frozen ball of dough in the microwave—again, at the lowest possible setting. Stop the microwave every few minutes to make sure the dough is not cooking. Sometimes, over-thawing in the microwave can result in dough that is very soft, clay-like, and almost TOO easy to work, and in which the yeast has been murdered by the heat so it doesn't rise. All is not lost. You can still get a delicious pizza out of that dough. The crust might not inflate the way you like it, and it might be chewier than usual.

HOW MUCH DOUGH?

This depends on how thick and how big you want the pizza to be. A dough ball that's on the heavy side of half a pound will press out nicely and not too thin to around 10 inches. A one-pound dough ball will press out to between 14 and 16 inches. If you want a thinner crust, use a smaller amount of dough.

> All the recipes in this book are written for a 14 -16 inch pizza and a one-pound pizza crust.

SHAPE YOUR DOUGH!

You can shape your dough on any flat, even surface—a large pan, a bread board or your countertop. The dough has a mind of its own, and sometimes it wants to go in a different direction than you do. The result can be a pizza that is oval, square, trapezoidal, shaped like any one of the 50 states or seven continents … anything but round.

When you want a round pizza, you can shape the dough in a pizza or cake pan whose diameter is about the same size as the pizza you want to make. The size and shape of the pan will give you a round crust.

Wherever you shape the dough, use a combination of PRESSING the dough out with your fingers towards the edges and carefully picking up the dough and STRETCHING it by:

PINCHING the edge between your thumbs and forefingers while rotating it … and

PULLING it out with your knuckles by supporting the dough on the flat knuckle-side of your clenched fists and slowly moving your fists apart, stretching the dough a bit, then rotating it and stretching again. (This happens to be the starting maneuver of a pizza toss, so it's worth practicing.)

WORK SURFACE—FLOUR OR OIL?

Your first opportunity to get some olive oil on your pizza is when pressing out the crust, by pouring olive oil on whatever surface you use. (The olive oil is good for your skin, too.)

Another option is to sift flour on the spreading surface and add olive oil later. The flour method might be the better method if your dough is on the wetter or gooier side.

DON'T use a rolling pin to stretch out your dough! It's easier but it presses all the air out of the dough, so you wind up with a cracker-like crust, not a chewy, bready crust. Making pizza is a sensual experience. Your hands will be oily one minute and caked with flour or dough the next. Get into it and enjoy it!

CHEESE!

You can use ANY cheese on ANY pizza. Some cheeses you wouldn't expect to find on a pizza work really well, like goat cheese, mild cheddars, jacks, and pepper cheeses. If stronger cheeses make your mouth water, like Italian table cheeses, French cheeses, or feta, go for it! Drier, harder cheeses tend not to melt as well as softer cheeses, but where is it written that pizza cheese has to melt?

Most pizzas in the world, and in this book, are adorned with mozzarella, or "mozz" (pronounced "mootz"). There are SO MANY varieties of mozzarella—fresh, shredded, part skim. I've had good luck with all varieties. You can buy it pre-shredded or shred your own in the food processor or the old fashioned way, with a cheese grater.

A lot of people get excited about fresh mozzarella, but a lot of the fresh mozzarella I've used has melted into a watery mess on the pizza. Some folks don't mind an extra juicy pizza. Neapolitan pizzas are juicy to the point of soupy. You eat them with a knife and fork. Still, there is fresh mozzarella out there (usually packed in shrink wrap, not soaking in water) that melts without flooding the pizza. Whether or not fresh mozzarella offers a flavor advantage worthy of the cost is your personal decision. Remember **Bosco's Prime Pizza Directive**: **Just get it DELICIOUS!**

TOMATOES!

Sauce is something that has been simmered for an hour or more to allow meat and other flavors to develop. If you want that, go for it. I like to use either fresh tomato slices, *crushed tomatoes*, or *whole tomatoes*—usually out of a can. The flavor I want to get out of the tomatoes on my pizzas is a bright, fruity burst, not a heavy, cooked sensation.

I usually get two or three pizzas out of a 28-ounce can of tomatoes. I drain the puree (and save it for soup or spaghetti sauce) and blend the whole tomatoes in a processor—with two or three tablespoons of olive oil, a teaspoon of garlic powder, a sprinkle of rosemary, and a pinch of salt. From the processor, it goes into a glass canning jar with a plastic lid. When I'm in a big hurry, I use a can of crushed tomatoes.

Speaking of salt, this is as good a time as any for a few words about …

The JOY of GRILL PIZZA!

SALT!

Most restaurant pizzas are salt bombs. The cheese is salty, the tomatoes are salty, even the dough is salty. The delayed salt reaction hits an hour or so after you eat, and you get crossing-the-desert thirsty.

Personally, I don't like salty food and I do try to keep the sodium level in my pizzas under control by using less salt or using lite salt. Having said that, you should know that sometimes all you need to do to give your pizza that professional "bite" and "brightness" is to sprinkle salt on it before you slice it.

GARLIC!

I couldn't live without garlic powder! Most of the time, I'm too lazy to peel, slice, and prepare fresh garlic. When I MUST have fresh garlic, I usually resort to the pre-peeled raw cloves. I sauté sliced or whole cloves in … you guessed it, olive oil.

GRATED CHEESE!

Grated cheese can be Parmesan, Romano, Pecorino, Locatelli … or some personal favorite. I try different types and brands and find joy in them all—even

the vacuum-packed bottles of Parmesan and Romano I grew up with and which my aunts still favor. Whatever

27

you use, the best time to sprinkle grated cheese on your pizza is just before you slice it.

FRESH BASIL!

Don't put the fresh basil on the pizza until AFTER it's cooked! It'll just shrivel and turn black. Strategically place your basil leaves on the pizza *before* sprinkling grated cheese, if you want the snowed-upon look, or *after* sprinking the cheese if you want the full green basil look.

> **Your pizza-lovin life is about to change FOREVER! You will NEVER think of pizza quite the same way AGAIN!**

Now ... Your First Grill Pizza!!!

When your dough is all pressed out and ready ... take a deep breath and ...

STEP I

LIGHT YOUR GRILL.

How hot should it be? Every grill is different. "Medium" on my grill could be "Scorchin!" on my neighbor's or "Brrr ... are you kiddin?" on yours. I usually light the grill and

The JOY of GRILL PIZZA!

set it at HIGH. If I have a lot of prepping to do for other pizzas and I can't give full attention to the pizza on the grill, I crank it down to MEDIUM when I place the pizza on the grill. As you get more experienced and relaxed with grill pizza, you'll find the best settings for your grill. For now, start with MEDIUM heat. Then, while the grill is heating up …

STEP 2

ASSEMBLE YOUR INGREDIENTS AND TOOLS NEAR THE GRILL.

Grill pizza chefs need to have a firm grasp of *mese en place,* which is French for, "lining up all your ingredients and tools in the correct order and position, so you have them WHEN and WHERE you need them."

So, your workstation should include all your ingredients in ready-to-spread condition, spoons, knives, or forks to spread them, a grill spatula or small pizza peel, and a bottle of olive oil with a pour spout or an olive oil sprayer, a water spritzer, and whatever else you might need or usually have near your grill.

STEP 3

WHEN THE GRILL IS READY, LIFT YOUR FLATTENED DOUGH OFF THE WORK SURFACE AND GINGERLY—BUT CAREFULLY—LAY IT ON THE GRILL.

D ON'T WORRY! It will NOT fall through the cracks! It will NOT burst into flames!

Most likely the dough will STRETCH as you lift it and lay it down, so it's NOT going to be quite the same shape

as it was before. For me, this is part of the fun of grill pizza— you never know what shape pizza is going to come out.

If you want perfectly round pizza, there are two things you can do. First, you can use a well-floured pizza peel to transfer the dough to the grill. OR, you can FREEZE your perfectly round dough in a plastic bag and lay a stiff but perfectly round circle of dough on the grill.

Option #1: Pour olive oil over the dough. If the dough had been shaped on a floured surface, you should definitely pour or spray some oil on the top. Two or three tablespoons should be plenty.

Option #2: Close the lid. I do this when it's cold outside or if I use frozen dough. I recommend you NOT close the lid until you have some experience and confidence in how long before The Flipping Point.

STEP 4

WATCH AND WAIT FOR THE FLIPPING POINT!

Huh?

The JOY of GRILL PIZZA!

WHAT'S THE FLIPPING POINT?

The Flipping Point is the Moment of Truth, the sweet spot when the dough is halfway to becoming a pizza crust. It's the moment when what is now the bottom is cooked enough to be flipped into position to become the TOP of your mouthwatering grill pizza.

This is where it gets emotional. Until you know how your grill treats pizza dough, you're going to imagine the dough instantly turning to charcoal or catching fire or dripping between the grates into the fire. Unless you're a total firebug or your grill goes nuclear, it's NOT GOING TO HAPPEN!

WHAT ARE YOU LOOKING FOR?

Three wonderful things are going to happen:

1 If you poured olive oil on top, it will eventually collect in pools and start sizzling. Mmmmm!

2 What is now the underside of the dough is going to be cooked by the grill. It will brown and develop grill marks AND some delicious char.

3 What is now the topside of the dough will also change. It will do what bread does when baked— rise. You'll see dough bubbles large and small. Maybe one HUGE dough bubble will inflate until your pizza looks like a basketball! NEVER FEAR! This is a GOOD THING!

If you've left the grill open, this will all happen before your eyes. Take pictures. This is an historic moment AT LEAST as important as Baby's First Step.

What you're looking for is how cooked the BOTTOM is. From time to time, lift a corner with the spatula and

look underneath.

This is a matter of personal taste, but at the very least you want light brown with darker grill marks. I look for a bottom that is lightly charred with brown to black grill marks and chars here and there on the bottom. Chances are that ONE MINUTE won't be enough, except for a very hot gas grill or a charcoal grill. So check again in another minute.

Keep checking until you see a bottom crust that looks good to you. Don't worry if it takes 3, 4, or 5 or more minutes. (With a charcoal grill, it will cook a LOT faster!)

IF YOU'VE CLOSED THE GRILL: If you're using a gas grill, wait ONE minute before you check and then check again at 30-second intervals.

If you're using a charcoal grill, wait HALF a minute and then check at 15–30 second intervals.

STEP 5—THE FLIPPING POINT!

WHEN THE BOTTOM IS DONE TO YOUR LIKING, FLIP THE PIZZA CRUST!

If you've got a 16-inch pizza to flip and you DON'T have a large grill spatula, you are now going to understand why I recommend one.

The JOY of GRILL PIZZA!

If you poured olive oil on top, it might FLAME UP as it spills on the fire or coals. If you've put off cleaning your grill and there's gunk in the bottom, you could see a bit of a GRILL FIRE here. DON'T PANIC! I keep a squirt bottle of water near the grill to spritz on grill fires.

Just don't get water on the PIZZA, PLEASE!

STEP 6

SPREAD YOUR TOPPINGS ON THE HOT PIZZA CRUST TOP.

Here is where speed counts. First, CHEESE, so the hot crust will melt it. The melted cheese provides an ooey-gooey anchor for whatever you put on top.

Then dollops of TOMATO. Then the rest of the CHEESE.

Option #1: Drizzle more OLIVE OIL.

Option #2: A snowstorm of GARLIC powder.

Option #3: A light sprinkle of fresh or dried rosemary.

The JOY of GRILL PIZZA!

> If you are using a VERY HOT GRILL or making a pizza with lots of toppings, it's okay to take it OFF THE GRILL and bring it back to your work surface to give yourself a bit more time to place the toppings without worrying about burning the bottom. Then, when you're done placing the toppings, return it to the grill and...

STEP 7

CLOSE THE LID.

BE BRAVE! You can turn the grill down a bit to give whatever you pile on top of the pizza time to heat up and/or melt before the bottom of the crust burns.

STEP 8

CHECK THE PIZZA AT ONE-MINUTE INTERVALS, 15-30 SECOND INTERVALS ON A CHARCOAL GRILL.

$\mathbf{N}$ow the waiting and checking start again. You're looking for the same thing as in Step 4—a nicely grilled bottom.

You also want the cheese to melt, but the condition of the bottom is more critical— you don't want it to get too charred.

Of course, everyone likes a different degree of char. One person's "just right" is another person's "burnt beyond recognition" is another person's "just a wee bit more, please!" I tend to prefer the blacker end of the char continuum. I've eaten pizzas that looked positively burnt and really loved them.

When the pizza bottom looks the way you want it ...

STEP 9

TRANSFER THE PIZZA TO THE SERVING PLATE.

$\mathbf{H}$ere is where a good-sized spatula really earns its keep. If your utensil is too small, it's no fun to balance a hot and juicy pizza on its way from the grill to the plate.

The JOY of GRILL PIZZA!

STEP 10

SLICE AND ENJOY THE BEST PIZZA YOU EVER TASTED!

Option #1: Sprinkle grated cheese.
Option #2: Arrange half a dozen or more basil leaves.

Wanna Try A Two-Flip Pizza?

All of the pizzas in this book are One-Flips, except the Real Grill Pizza on page 4 and this page. To get the thick corniche look of that pizza, try a Two-Flip pizza. You'll add just one step. Call it Step 4A.

To make a Two-Flip Pizza, keep the first side down JUST LONG ENOUGH to let the top get bubbly and uneven while the bottom gets JUST firm enough to flip. That first flip will come a lot sooner. Check more frequently and when the bottom JUST STARTS TO DEVELOP LIGHT BROWN GRILL MARKS and the dough is cooked firm enough to turn, FLIP IT. That's the extra step.

Now let the "bumpy" side stay down long enough to get nice and cooked, with grill marks and chars the way you like'em.

Then pick up the process at Step 5, the main Flipping Point. Flip the pizza, place your toppings, and close the grill. EASY as PIZZA PIE!

Now that you know how to make the best pizza you ever tasted, it's time to throw a grill pizza party!

Pizza is a food that brings people together. There *are* things called "personal pizzas" but they are the exception. The rule is: You enjoy pizza in the company of others, relaxed, having a good time.

Pizza is a natural for the grill and the kind of meal grills usually create. You can even grill your toppings before you put them on the pizza.

The JOY of GRILL PIZZA!

Grill Pizza Is as American as Mom's Apple Pie Pizza

T he French are obsessive about cooking technique. The Italians are obsessive about ingredients. For better or worse, we Americans don't have a lot of patience with either obsession. For worse, this results in a lot of really awful American food. For better, our freedom to combine ingredients and alter techniques gives us an unmatched ability to discover new flavors and improve on the classics.

That's what I've tried to do with my recipes—and it's what I encourage you to do with yours. Try new things, new ingredients, new combinations of ingredients, so that at least once every pizza party someone says to you:

"You put WHAT on top of that pizza?"

You Put *WHAT* on Top of That Pizza?

K eep reminding yourself that though some elements of cooking are fairly precise chemistry—the difference between great dough and throw-away dough can be a couple of grams of yeast or degrees variation in temperature—grill pizza is not. Once you have your dough, you have a LOT of latitude in how you grill and dress your pizza. Your grill is not only forgiving of your wild, impulsive ways, but generous in its favors. So…

If you want a charred pizza, crank up the grill and leave the pizza on longer.

If you want a lighter crust, turn down the fire and flip the pizza sooner.

If you want a cheesier pizza, pile it on!

Whatever ingredients tempt your taste buds, go for it!

And please let me know how your pizzas come out. Send your outrageously delicious recipes, photos, and comments to:

YouPutWHATonTopofthatPIZZA@
TheJoyOfGrillPizza.com

You Put *WHAT* on Top of That Pizza?

Grill Pizza Recipes

The most fun I EVER had working on this book (or any other) was creating, testing, and photographing the recipes—with the help of Jane and Susan. The recipes that follow are just your jumping off point into a new world of pizza.

All the recipes in this book
are written for a 14 -16 inch pizza
and a one-pound pizza crust.

The ONLY Universal Rule For Grill Pizza Ingredients:

All ingredients should be edible and near, at, or above room temperature at the time they go on top of the pizza!

So saute it, roast it, or GRILL IT before it goes on that pizza!

Bosco's Prime Pizza Directive

Just GET IT DELICIOUS!

Use the ingredients that taste good to YOU! Go with the easiest and most convenient options that will give you the flavors you love.

NOT QUITE A VIRGIN

**1/2 cup crushed tomatoes (see Classic Maggie
for recipe)
3 teaspoons Romano or Parmesan cheese
sprinkled over pizza
drizzle olive oil
optional: fresh basil leaves or dollar bills**

Two of my most vivid and deliciously haunting food memories come from childhood visits to The Feast, which was an Italian carnival in honor of the Assumption of the Madonna, every August in New Haven. This pizza honors the first of these memories,

The Knights of Columbus always made fried *apizza* in a huge caldron over a fire. They boiled the dough in oil, ladeled on marinara sauce and sprinkled the *apizza* with cheese. Heaven!

Later, these same men led a procession through the Feast carrying a huge painting of the Virgin Mary festooned with hundreds, maybe THOUSANDS, of dollar bills.

This is the easiest pizza to make. Just flip it, ladel on the crushed tomatoes, drizzle some extra olive oil, and then sprinkle the grated cheese and extra garlic powder.

The JOY of GRILL PIZZA!

LA FESTA—THE FEAST

6–8 oz mozzarella
1 pound Italian sausage (hot or sweet)
4 medium peppers (green, red, yellow, or orange)
1 large yellow onion
6 cloves garlic

We always went to The Feast at night, and it was always deliciously scary and thrilling at the same time. The men from the Mary Magdalene Society sold incredibly delicious sausage and peppers sandwiches from a stand near the scary-high Ferris wheel.

Slice the onion, garlic, and peppers and sauté with the sausage in 2–3 tablespoons of olive oil.

THE CHICKEN CAPER

**8 oz mozzarella, shredded or sliced
2 chicken breasts, thin-sliced
1/4 cup all-purpose flour
3 tablespoons olive oil
6–10 oz artichoke hearts
3 teaspoons capers, drained
3 teaspoons butter
6 cloves garlic, sliced
1 teaspoon lemon juice
1 teaspoon red pepper flakes**

Chicken Scallopini fans love this pizza! Coat the chicken in flour, salt, and pepper. Sauté in olive oil over medium heat until golden brown and slice into chunks. Add capers, artichoke hearts, garlic, lemon juice, butter, red pepper flakes and sauté until heated through.

NOT YOUR FATHER'S PEPPERONI PIZZA

6–8 oz shredded or sliced mozzarella
I cup thick-sliced pepperoni
1/2 cup crushed tomatoes
1/4 cup garlic slices or chunks
6–8 oz bacon

Sauté the garlic with the bacon. Break or cut the bacon slices into pieces about an inch long and spread on the pizza after the tomatoes but before any cheese you've saved for the top.

I ate enough as pepperoni as a kid to last a lifetime. I ate it by the STICK, not the slice! I was never a fan of pepperoni pizza, though. But my friends and pizza party guests always asked for a pepperoni pizza … so, not wanting to disappoint them, I had to make a pie that was intense enough to make me want to eat pepperoni pizza. I did it, if I do say so myself. Pass the pepperoni pizza!

THE WOOSTER STREET

6–8 oz fresh mozzarella
1 1/2 cup Italian home fries
8 cloves garlic, sautéed
1 medium onion
drizzle olive oil
sprinkle fresh or dried rosemary
sprinkle garlic powder
sprinkle grated cheese

This pizza salutes the seasonal potato pizza served at Sally's on Wooster Street in New Haven. To make the Italian home fries, I cut half a dozen medium potatoes into mostly perfect disks and sautéed them in olive oil with 8 cloves of garlic and a sliced medium onion. I wound up with a frying pan of perfect potato disks and an ungainly rag-tag of fried potato chunks. I collected the rag-tag chunks and used *them* on the pizza instead of the perfect disks. There's no accounting for visual taste, either!

I DID IT MY WAY

6–8 oz mozzarella
1 can baby clams, drained
6 cloves garlic, sliced (or not)
1 teaspoon Italian spice mix
8 oz bacon, broken up
1/4 cup Italian bread crumbs (or panko)
grated cheese sprinkled on top

Sauté the clams with the garlic and spices. Add the bread crumbs or panko to the sautéed clams or sprinkle them on the pizza at the end. Because so much grease cooks out of bacon, sauté that separately.

I named this pizza in honor of my dad, Joe, whose favorite song was *I Did It My Way*. Dad also loved clamming and casinos.

THE JANE-JANE OMG!!!!

1/2 cup mango chutney
6 oz Asiago cheese
6–8 garlic cloves, sliced and sautéed
1 pork chop or loin, cooked with rosemary
and cubed (or 6 strips cooked bacon)

Whenever a pizza has both cheese and a somewhat gooey ingredient, like chutney, you have a dilemma. The chutney would be easier to spread evenly if you put it on FIRST, before the cheese. But, then, will the cheese melt? I've tried it both ways, and, usually, the cheese DOES melt.

Jane wanted a pizza people could make with leftovers—in this case, pork chops. The first time we tried it, the first words out of her mouth after her first bite were *Oh my God!* Hence, the name. The plot thickened a week later when I made one but, because I didn't happen to have any pork chops, leftover or otherwise, used bacon. My daughter Giulianna LOVED it! For her, this pizza MUST be made with bacon. For Jane, pork chops!

TACO BELLA

6–8 oz shredded Pepper Jack cheese
1 cup cooked ground beef/turkey
1/2 cup taco sauce
1/2 cup diced tomatoes
1 cup shredded lettuce
1/2 cup diced scallions

serve with salsa and a dollop of sour cream

First time we tried to make a taco pizza, it was good but not great. It was missing something. Susan suggested taco sauce. Why didn't I think of that? It's just what the pizza needed! I confess, I seldom eat tacos. But this pizza is Something Else Entirely!

ED'S PORTUGUEE MAN-O-WAR PIZZA

6–8 oz mozzarella, sliced or shredded
1 pound of Portuguese chourico
1 medium onion, sliced
6 cloves of garlic
2 cans of clams, drained
1/2 cup of white wine or beer
2 teaspoons sugar
ungodly amounts of olive oil

Slice the chourico, the onion, and the garlic and brown in olive oil. Then add wine (or beer), clams, and sugar and boil down to a thick stew consistency, stirring frequently. Half the cheese goes on the pizza first, then the chourico/clams "stew," then, finally, more cheese.

This recipe was a real test for my Prime Pizza Directive. Jane provided this recipe as it was handed down by her father, Ed. Originally it was served with crusty French bread and required fresh mussels or littleneck clams stewed in the shell with onions, garlic, and wine or beer.

Since I don't do fresh mussels or clams, I resorted to canned baby clams. Would Jane approve? Well, I delivered it to her house before she got home. An hour or so later, she called: *Wow! Best pizza you EVER MADE!*

I LEFT MY ARTICHOKE HEARTS IN SAN FRANCISCO: VEGGIE

6–8 oz shredded or sliced mozzarella
1 can artichoke hearts drained and sliced
2–3 cups roasted or grilled veggies
sliced or crushed black olives
drizzle olive oil

This pizza can be different every time you make it. It's a veggie free-for-all! You can grill some eggplant, squash, onions, peppers … whatever you like! Or sauté them in olive oil, garlic, balsamic vinegar, and a little sugar. Some stores even carry frozen bags of already roasted or grilled veggies, so all you have to do is thaw 'em and you're ready for pizza!

SHRIMP-A-LUSCIOUS

6-8 oz shredded or sliced mozzarella
1/2–1 pound shrimp
1 teaspoon red pepper flakes
1/2 cup scallions
1 tablespoon grated cheese

I used peeled cooked extra large shrimp on this pizza. I prepped them by sautéing 6–8 sliced garlic cloves in olive oil, mixing in the red pepper flakes and Italian spices from the spice grinder (oregano, rosemary, onion, parsley), and then JUST WARMING the already-cooked shrimp in the pan. You don't want to heat it to the point of becoming tough! If you start with peeled raw shrimp, sauté them until fully cooked. Remember: Don't depend on ANYTHING cooking on top of the pizza!

Sprinkle the grated cheese and diced scallions on the finished pizza.

I LEFT MY ARTICHOKE HEARTS IN SAN FRANCISCO: PESTO

1 cup pesto
1 can artichoke hearts drained and sliced
6–8 oz shredded or sliced mozzarella
1/2 cup crushed black olives

I had my first pesto pizza in San Francisco, not far from the corner of Haight and Ashbury. I purposely do not include a recipe for pesto, because pesto is one of those foods where everybody swears by his or her absolute favorite. This pizza will work with ANY kind of pesto. Spread the pesto FIRST and then the cheese.

MEAT YOU ALL THE WAY

8 oz extra sharp cheese, shredded
4–8 oz leftover steak or roast beef, well-seasoned
1 medium onion, sliced and sautéed
6 cloves garlic, sliced and sautéed

Apologies to Roseanna. This pizza always gets rave reviews, but no one liked the original name, *The Steak Bomb*.

The ABSOLUTE BEST steaks I ever ate were the chuck steaks my father cooked on his makeshift grill (cinder blocks and an old stove grate) in the back yard. The problem with using grilled steaks to make this pizza is that there are never any leftovers when you grill steaks. So … if you don't have leftover steak, use roast beef given a quick sauté in olive oil and garlic powder. Actually, sautéing in garlic and olive oil boosts the flavor of leftover steak, too.

POPEYE AND OLIVE OIL

6–8 oz shredded or sliced mozzarella
2 cups cooked/well-drained spinach
2 teaspoons olive oil
2 teaspoons garlic powder (or 6 cloves fresh garlic)
1/4 teaspoon salt
1 cup black olives, crushed or sliced
diced red pepper for color

The spinach must be SUPER well-drained, to the point of SQUEEZING most of the water out of it! You don't want a soggy pizza! Mix the spinach with olive oil, garlic, and salt. You want the spinach to really make an impression when you take your first bite. So make sure you cram lots of garlicky flavor into it BEFORE you put it on the pizza.

FRENCH HERESY

8 oz Brie, sliced or shredded
1 medium almost-carmelized onion, sliced
dried cranberries
2 tablespoons butter
2 tablespoons white balsamic vinegar
2–3 tablespoons light brown sugar
1/4 cup walnut pieces

The heresy here is using French cuisine's two or three most prized ingredients ON A PIZZA! I don't know, is it just me or is French cuisine just a little too ANAL? Lighten UP, *mes amis!* If you want to compound the crime, enjoy this pizza with BEER!

Then … how do you "almost-carmelize" an onion? Slice it and sauté it in a couple of tablespoons of olive oil, balsamic vinegar and light brown sugar until it starts to brown—but remove from the heat before it gets all soft and gooey. Sauté the walnuts in the butter and sprinkle over the finished pizza.

RIKKI TIKKI PIZZA

1/2–3/4 cup ricotta cheese
6–8 oz Masala sauce
3 tablespoons sugar
chicken strips or chunks, sautéed.
2–4 oz Monterey Jack cheese, shredded

I HAD to have an Indian Pizza! Chicken Masala is a big favorite in our family. Since I find it at every Indian buffet I've ever seen, it must be pretty popular. Most supermarkets carry Masala sauce, too.

After you brown the chicken, add the Masala sauce and sugar and let the mixture simmer for several minutes.

REUBEN NEVER HAD IT SO GOOD!

4–8 oz corned beef
6–8 oz Swiss cheese, sliced
4–6 oz sauerkraut
1/4–1/2 cup Thousand Island dressing
several healthy squirts of Dijon mustard
1 tablespoon caraway seeds

I used sliced deli corn beef for this pizza, but if you have some leftover boiled corn beef and cabbage, use that and call it an Irish Pizza! (To boost the flavor of deli meat for a pizza, I briefly sauté it in garlic and olive oil.) I drained the sauerkraut so it wouldn't make the crust soggy. Be sure to save a few slices of cheese for the top!

GENERAL TSO'S PIZZA

4–6 oz mozzarella, shredded
6 oz chicken chunks, sautéed in olive oil with
4 oz General Tso's sauce, and
1/2 cup broccoli, diced (optional)
1/2 cup scallions, diced

Part of the joy of grill pizza is being able to build a pizza out of your favorite foods. Well, General Tso's chicken is one of my daughter Giulianna's favorites, so here it is. You can use take-out General Tso's, which usually includes broccoli, or make your own.

There is probably no Chinese take-out that wouldn't make an interesting and delicious pizza. Send your concoctions to:

YouPutWHATonTopOfThatPizza@TheJoyofGrillPizza.com

PORTA-PALOOZA

2 teaspoons mayonnaise
6–8 oz mozzarella, shredded or sliced
6–8 oz portabello mushroom slices
1 medium orange pepper (or red or green or yellow), diced
7–10 cloves fresh garlic sliced
drizzle olive oil

Sauté the portabello slices and garlic in olive oil. Add the diced pepper about halfway through. The diced pepper was originally added for color, but we discovered that it provided a nice flavor and a chewy texture with the mushrooms.

POLE IN A GRASS SKIRT

6–8 oz smoked mozzarella, shredded
4 oz sweet and sour sauce
2 tablespoons soy sauce or teriyaki sauce
6–10 oz kielbasa, sliced and browned in olive oil
4–6 cloves garlic, sliced (optional)
1 can pineapple chunks (or crushed) well-drained, lightly browned

Brown the kielbasa and garlic in olive oil, then add sweet and sour sauce and soy sauce. After removing the kielbasa, you can throw the drained pineapple chunks in the pan to pick up some of the brownish-red color and saucy flavor.

Spread most of the cheese first, then a few dollops of sauce. After adding the kielbasa and pineapple, add the rest of the cheese and sauce.

BRAVO AVOCADO!

4–6 oz Monterey Jack cheese or mild cheddar, shredded
6–10 strips, thick-sliced bacon
1 avocado, sliced
1 tomato, sliced

So easy to make! The hardest part is cooking the bacon and breaking it into smaller pieces.

This pizza makes such a delicious breakfast or brunch! It's one of those pizzas that looks too good to eat—but that won't stop you.

Remember to save some of the cheese to sprinkle on top.

The JOY of GRILL PIZZA!

BREAKFAST IN OLD TOWN

4 oz Monterey Jack cheese shredded
1 cup refried beans
6–8 eggs, fried sunny side up
1/2 cup salsa

The first time I had *huevos rancheros* was at an outdoor restaurant in Old Town San Diego. Maybe it was the balmy sunshine on a Southern California November morning … maybe it was the romance of Old Town … maybe it was that the chef really knew his *huevos*. Whatever it was, I was instantly hooked. I think you will be, too.

The trick with this pizza is HOW to cook the eggs and WHEN to put them on the pizza. Sunny-side-up definitely makes for a prettier pizza. I put the Jack cheese on first, then the refried beans, then carefully transferred the eggs from the frying pan to the top of the pizza while it was on the grill. I closed the grill top for about two minutes. If your grill throws a lot of heat and you DON'T want the eggs to dry out, add them after the bottom of the pizza is done.

HOLY GUACAMOLE!

6–8 oz Monterey Jack cheese shredded
4–8 oz guacamole
1 medium (red or sweet) onion, thin-sliced
fresh tomato, cut into chunks

Which should you spread on the crust first, the cheese or the guacamole? I almost always spread the cheese first, so the hot crust can melt it. With this pizza, after the cheese was down, I spooned on the guacamole. I had to jerk the spoon a bit each time. You won't be able to cover every square inch with guacamole, but that's okay. It will melt and spread a bit.

MANGO-TANGO (AKA THE BRONX CHEER BREAKFAST PIZZA)

mango-orange sauce:
3/4 cup mango preserves
3 tablespoons orange juice
I tablespoon corn starch

1/2–I pint fresh raspberries

drizzle 1/2 cup glaze:
I tablespoon melted butter
3 tablespoons milk
1/2 cup confectioner's sugar

I cup walnut pieces

Though it could be considered a dessert pizza, we call it a breakfast pizza because when we developed and tested the recipe, several of our testers had given up dessert for Lent, so they couldn't eat anything called "dessert."

To make the mango sauce, mix 3/4 cup mango preserves with 3 tablespoons orange juice and 1 tablespoon corn starch. Stir well, then microwave on HIGH for 20-30 seconds and stir again. To make the white glaze, mix 1/2 cup confectioner's sugar with 1 tablespoon melted butter and 3 teaspoons milk.

The mango sauce goes on first, then the raspberries, then the glaze, then the walnuts.

LOVE ON A SATURDAY MORNING

4 oz Monterey Jack cheese, shredded
3–5 eggs, scrambled
7 strips of thick-sliced bacon

People usually associate things like flowers and chocolates with love. Me? I associate the smell of bacon and eggs. When I woke up on Saturday morning and smelled bacon and eggs, it meant my dad was in the kitchen cooking breakfast.

The JOY of GRILL PIZZA!

LICENSE TO PRINT MONEY

3 oz coconut milk syrup
8–10 mango slices
mint leaves (place before serving)

I discovered Thai Coconut Sticky Rice with Mango slices at a street fair in San Rafael, California. The line was so long at the booth selling it that a movie business friend remarked that it was a license to print money. I agreed.

The first time I made one of these, I added a quarter cup of sugar and a tablespoon of corn starch to an 8 oz can of coconut milk and boiled it down into a thick syrup. Then I discovered coconut syrup at the supermarket!

If fresh, ripe mangoes aren't available, try canned or bottled mango slices, which is what I used for this photo.

S'MORE PIZZA PLEASE!!!!!!!!

4–6 oz marshmallow creme (and/or marshmallows)
3 tablespoons melted butter
1/4 cup light brown sugar
1 cup crushed and broken graham crackers
1/2 cup chocolate chips or chunks
maraschino cherries

Whenever I make this dessert pizza at a party, it goes FAST!

Melt the butter, then stir in the brown sugar to make the syrup. After flipping the pizza crust, spread the marshmallow crème first, then the melted butter/brown sugar syrup. Drop most of the chocolate chips evenly across the pzza, then the graham crackers, then the rest of the chocolate chips. Don't worry if the chocolate chips don't appear to melt. They usually hold their shape even when melted. In the pictured pizza, I placed whole marshmallows, sliced in half, on top of larger graham cracker pieces, and then topped them off with maraschino cherries.

CHEESECAKE SUSAN'S

1 cup cream cheese
1/2 cup sugar
2 cups cherry pie filling
1/2 cup chocolate chips or chunks
drizzle brandy before serving (optional)

We made this pizza on Valentine's Day, to top off an evening of testing and photographing pizzas. Even though we were all quite happily full, this one disappeared within minutes.

Mix or whip the cream cheese with the sugar before spreading. If you use tart cherries, balance the sweetness and tartness by using milk chocolate chips. If you use sweet cherries, use semi-sweet chocolate chips.

Variations: Try Marscapone cheese, ricotta, or even cottage cheese in place of the cream cheese. ANY fruit will do: strawberries, raspberries, blueberries, even bananas!

MOM'S APPLE PIE

1 cup cream cheese
1/2 cup brown sugar and
1/2 teaspoon cinnamon
2 cups apple pie filling

1 cup walnut pieces or pecan pieces
dried cranberries

1/2 cup icing (before serving):
1 tablespoon melted butter
3 tablespoons milk
1 teaspoon vanilla extract
1/2 cup confectioner's sugar

Mix together the cream cheese, brown sugar , and cinnamon That mixture goes on the pizza first. Then the apple pie filling. Then the walnut or pecan pieces and dried cranberries. Top off the pizza with white icing, made with 1/2 cup confectioner's sugar mixed with 1 tablespoon melted butter, vanilla, and 3 teaspoons milk.

ON FIRE FOR YOU

5 medium bananas
1/4 cup butter
1/4 cup light brown sugar or honey
1/4 cup banana liqeuer
1/4 cup high octane rum
serve with vanilla ice cream

This pizza gave me the chance to realize my worst fear and most thrilling fantasy—to see a grill pizza engulfed in flames! Bananas Foster is a real show-stopper at dinner parties. So why not a grill pizza version? In a frying pan I sautéed 5 sliced bananas with butter and brown sugar, added some banana liqueur, and brought the mixture back to simmering. Meanwhile, the pizza crust was on the grill. I carried the pan with the hot bananas-sugar-liqeuer mixture out to the grill and stirred in the high-proof rum. I flipped the pizza and poured the hot bananas-sugar-rum mixture onto the top. Then I lit it. The trick was to get it on the pizza and light it before all the alcohol evaporated. As you can see, I succeeded.

The JOY of Grill Pizza

Pizza is as good a metaphor for life as anything I've ever come across. Maybe even a little better than most.

While working on this book, I had a day when making pizza was the last thing I wanted to do. I had enough dough in the fridge for three pizzas— a big bubbling bowl of it that really needed using. But the dough smelled a little on the winey side. I knew that sometimes winey dough can be a disaster. But I pressed on, literally, pressing the dough into shape.

Winey wasn't the only problem this dough had. Its texture was strange. Though made with bread flour, it didn't seem to have developed as much elasticity as it should have. It was a little on the mushy side. But I

knew the yeast was alive and kicking because there were bubbles in the dough.

When I placed the dough on the grill, it pulled apart in several places, and left a big coin-size hole in the crust. I shook my head and figured this was going to be a throwaway, but I left it on the grill, closed the lid, and went inside. (It was February, and COLD!)

A few minutes later, I went out, expecting to find a pizza crust I'd probably throw away. But the grilling dough actually smelled pretty good. The hole had charred through and when I flipped it, the grill marks looked nice and dark. Oh well. The cheese and sauce were out there anyway ... so I put them on and closed the lid.

When I took it off the grill, the pizza looked okay but nothing extraordinary. I sliced it up, chose a piece ... and took a bite.

What can I say to convey how surprised I was? For looks, this pizza was not even in the middle range of pizzas I've made. But in flavor, it was easily one of the best pizzas I ever tasted! I know it's not much to look at. But if you could taste it, you'd know why I had to include its photo.

Pizza, like life, is full of surprises. Not all of them delicious. But the delicious ones can restore your faith in … delicious surprises.

I almost threw away that dough. The crushed tomatoes were not the best money can buy, either. Nor was the cheese especially fresh. The olive oil cost a dime an ounce. But they all came together on the grill into something really amazing. It was a real *"Wow, I can't believe how good that tastes!"* experience.

That's why I wrote this book, to share with you the secrets of creating those delicious surprises in your own backyard.

That pizza reminded me what this book is about. You, too, will find yourself saying, over and over again, *"Wow, I can't believe how INCREDIBLE that tastes!"*

And right after you say that, you'll shake your head and say, *"I can't believe how EASY that was!"*

You'll think there is some kind of pizza magic at work—and you'll be right. It's magic that you can do, again and again. In your own backyard.

ACKNOWLEDGMENTS

Every book I've written has been done in solitude, except
this one, which started with a party, ended with party, felt
like a party in the middle, and promises parties to come.
For that, I am deeply grateful. Jane, Luther, Janna, Kaylee,
Maya, Chase, Susan, Brooks, Annah, Janet, Phil, Steven,
Melanie, Maura, Cody, Grace, Kim, Bruce, Julia, Eric,
Nick, Devin... you all came into my home and my life at
a good time and brought recipes, pizza toppings, and joy.
Luther, thanks for Kathy and your quiet but magnificent
generosity. Chase, bringer of light, my appreciation.
Susan Woolverton Rozelle, your enthusiasm and your
cooking smarts sure came in handy, and you take a great
picture, too.

And Jane-Jane Camara Moen, I don't know how you do it,
but I do know I couldn't have done it without you.

DB

The JOY of GRILL PIZZA!

CPSIA information can be obtained
at www.ICGtesting.com
Printed in the USA
LVIW010507280812

296244LV00001B